Today Arizona's cities, large and small bring a special feel to this diverse southwestern region. Cosmopolitan museums, art galleries, impressive sport's complexes, world-renowned educational and scientific research facilities bring both national and international acclaim to our state. On the roads less traveled, cattlemen and sheepherders can still be seen on wide open ranges tending their herds. Native Americans dwell atop towering mesas and deep canyon floors living much as their ancestors did hundreds of years ago. The natural, historical and cultural contrasts of this region are what make the great state of Arizona so amazing.

Cover Photo: Early winter morning at the San Francisco Peaks, Flagstaff.

AMAZING ARIZONA is a publication of Bob Bradshaw, P.O. Box 20062, Sedona, AZ 86341
Photography by Bob Bradshaw except where noted by Eldemira Portillo.

Text by Eldemira Portillo. Special thanks to Rita Garrett of A Day in the West, Media Center for assistance in the design and layout of "Amazing Arizona".

Printed in China through Four Colour Imports

ISBN 0-9629319-5-0

W9-CHC-315

1

Bob Bradshaw, whose award winning photography captures the timeless beauty and wonder of nature presents his latest book. "Amazing Arizona" will inspire you to explore Arizona's rich natural, historical and cultural diversity. Join Bob as he takes you on a photographic journey of the many scenic wonders of Arizona. Explore Arizona's canyons, mountains and river valleys of the high-low desert regions. Revisit the ways of ancient civilization and rediscover the pioneering spirit of the early settlers who shaped the history and character of the towns and cities that make Arizona so unique. As a major contributor to "Arizona Highways Magazine" for 35 years, Bob is a historian, rancher and contributor in many motion pictures and TV commercials filmed in Sedona and the Northland. He has published numerous books; "Westerns of the Red Rock County", "Sedona Red Rock Country", "Verde Valley's Hidden Treasures", "Indian Country", "Four Seasons of Sedona" and his autobiography "The Sedona Man". Well into his eighties, Bob Bradshaw has mastered with each click of his lens the ability to reawaken the longing man has to reconnect with nature.

© Eldemira Portillo

Standing next to petrified log at the Petrified National Forest, Eldemira Portillo, photographer under the guidance of Bob Bradshaw researched, designed, and wrote the copy for this publication. "Before meeting Bob Bradshaw, I approached nature in a very casual way. After spending several years learning photography from Bob, things changed for me. I will never look at a landscape in the same way again, it's been a life changing event".

3

# Hart Prairie

Discover the majestic views of the San Francisco Peaks from the numerous access roads along Hwy 180. The result of a succession of volcanic eruptions over a million years ago formed these peaks. The powerful forces of erosion and ice sculpted this dormant volcano to its present form. The landscape surrounding the peaks offers a rich display of biological diversity; ponderosa pines, fir, and spruce forests mingle with patches of aspen groves. The mountain floors are covered with ferns, lupine, columbine and the San Francisco groundsel; found nowhere else in the world. Elk, deer and wild turkey are commonly seen roaming the meadows at the base of these majestic mountains. Humphreys' Peak towers at an astonishing 12,643 feet, the highest in Arizona. Neighboring Native American tribes regard the San Francisco Peaks as sacred. The Hopi call them home of the Kachina Spirits and to the Navajo people the peaks mark a portion of the western Navajo Nation's boundary. The beauty and splendor of these mountains draw people from all walks of life seeking peace and solitude.

# Smidts Cabin

A colorful autumn day in Hart Prairie north of Flagstaff.

# The Grand Canyon

The Grand Canyon of the Colorado River remains unsurpassed as one of the world's seven natural wonders. The result of billions of years of erosion combined with the powerful forces of the Colorado River are etched into the sheer cliffs, plateaus and side canyons of this Grandest of Canyons. Over one mile deep, 277 miles long and up to ten miles wide, with elevations ranging from 1200 feet up to 9000 feet, the canyon encompasses a wide range of transitional zones. Home to an abundance of wildlife including the rare California condor and a wide range of plant species, both contribute to the vast biological diversity of this awe-inspiring region. Initially discovered in 1540 by Spanish explorer Francisco Vasquez de Coronado's expedition, while searching for the Seven Golden Cities of Cibola. The Grand Canyon was later explored by Major John Wesley Powell's expedition in 1869. With a crew of 9 boatmen and survey equipment, Major Powell braved the river's dynamic rapids exploring the length of this magnificent canyon. (Left) Rhododendrons line the North Rim of the Grand Canyon.

With an elevation 120[?] feet higher than the Sou[?] Rim, heavy snows close t[?] road to the North Rim fr[?] October to May. Entran[?] to the North Rim is throug[?] State Hwy 68 at Jac[?] Lake, where alpine fores[?] and meadows contrast t[?] pinion juniper forest on t[?] south rim. Here the rim [?] lined with ponderosa pir[?] fir, spruce and aspen fores[?]

From this vantage point visitors are afforded a remarkable view of the geological history of the Canyon. Each stratum of rock marks a period of earth's history, spanning 250 million to 2 billion years. Angel's Window, at Cape Royal lookout cuts through layers of redwall limestone.

# Grand Canyon's North Rim

The popular North Rim Canyon Trails allow hikers an opportunity to explore the many hidden side canyons.

# Grand Canyon's South Rim

The south rim of the Grand Canyon at an elevation of 7,000 feet yields plant species typical of a high desert region. Pinyon pine, juniper, sagebrush and the occasional agave cactus grace the canyon rim. The drive along the rim affords a series of incomparable views along it's 35 mile paved route.

A canyon visitor takes in the Grand Canyon
from this vantage point along the rim trail.

Eldemira Portillo

The south rim trail extends along the rim of the canyon between Maricopa Point and the Yavapai Museum. For a more leisurely canyon experience, this relatively flat 3.5 mile paved trail provides the casual tourist an intimate view of the canyon at their own pace.

The mood of the canyon constantly changes with the passing of clouds overhead.

# Monument Valley Navajo Tribal Park

Monument Valley with its dramatic sandstone mesas, buttes and spires is located on the Arizona ~ Utah border north of Kayenta. Witness the daily life of the colorful Navajo people tending their flocks of sheep among these sandy hills and sandstone monoliths. Sheep herding has been vital to the economic survival of the Navajo providing food and wool for past and future generations. Mutton Stew and frybread constitute a traditional Navajo meal. The highly sought after Navajo rugs are created from the sheep's wool, dyes from native plants and the ancient weaving skills of the Navajo women. Turquoise and silver jewelry designed by skilled artists and ceremonial sand paintings are displayed at many fine art galleries and museums in the Southwest.

Navajo mother and daughter ride below Ear of the Wind Arch, Monument Valley.

# Navajo Life

A lone Navajo sheepherder guides his flock to scarce water supplies and food.

# Navajo National Monument

Home to the Anasazi, Betatakin Ruins in Navajo National Monument demonstrates the amazing adaptability of these "Ancient Ones" to their surroundings. The cliff dwellings provided protection from the elements as well as hostile neighboring tribes.

# Canyon de Chelly

Canyon de Chelly National Monument three miles east of Chinle, was home to five periods of Native American cultures; the Archaic, Basketmakers, Anasazi, Hopi and the Navajo dating as far back as 2500 B.C. The Archaic, Basketmakers and the Anasazi occupied these canyons to 1350 A.D. The Hopi utilized them during the 14th and 15th centuries, with the Navajo arriving sometime in the 17th century.

The Navajo live along the canyon rim in the winter. During the summer months they occupy the twenty-six mile long canyon floor, where they grow corn, peaches and raise livestock.

The sandstone walls rising up to one thousand feet in places, are decorated with pictographs dating from the earliest settlers to the present Navajo occupation. Antelope House, Standing Cow, Mummy Cave and White House Ruin (pictured left) are the principal ruins. White House Ruin is the most accessible to hikers. Mummy Cave Ruin is one of the largest cliff dwellings in the country, it is not accessible to visitors because it's considered highly sacred to the Native American culture.

# Sunset Crater

Named after its fiery red crest that intensifies with the fading light of the setting sun, Sunset Crater erupted some 900 years ago. By studying the magnetism of the lava flows, scientists conclude that this magnificent crater formed from a series of eruptions spanning several hundred years.

This impressive cinder cone volcano rising 1000 feet is surrounded by a sea of frozen lava flows, rich with color and texture. Sunset Crater and a series of smaller cinder cones make up the San Francisco Volcanic Field. In this aerial photgraph the majestic snow capped San Francisco Peaks dominate the horizon.

# Walpi and Four Corners Monument

alpi, located on one of ree clusters of mesas erlooking the vast desert the oldest continuously habited site on the Hopi servation. Perched at e western tip of First esa, this sacred site has en called "home" by the opi for well over 1,100 ars. This rare photograph Walpi gives viewers a mpse of the Hopi way of e. No photography, painting, sketching or video recording is permitted on the Hopi land.

Four Corners Monument, depicted in this vintage photograph is located near the Navajo Trail Highway. It marks the only point in the United States common to four states: Arizona, Utah, Colorado and New Mexico.

# Glen Canyon National Recreation Area

This sweeping aerial view of Lake Powell shrouded by imposing storm clouds is a popular area for boating, fishing, camping and hiking. Ranked the second largest man-made reservoir in the nation, boasting 1,960 miles of shoreline and spanning well into southern Utah. The red hued cliffs surrounding this magnificent lake rise an impressive 400 feet above the waters surface in some places; forming the many hidden side canyons, sandy coves, and inlets for which Lake Powell is famous.

Beautiful striated sandstone cones can be seen at the entrance to the Glen Canyon Recreation Area, located 119 miles north of Flagstaff on US Hwy 89a.

# Glen Canyon Dam

Completed in 1963, Glen Canyon Dam near Page rises 710 feet from the canyon floor of what once was Glen Canyon. Impounding 27 million acre-feet of water, the dam regulates the release of flow into the Colorado River providing electrical power to neighboring cities.

# The Petrified Forest

The Petrified Forest south of I-40 near Holbrook is an outdoor display of petrified wood seemingly tumbled about mounds of colorful, striated rock formations. The trees burned over time, roughly some 180 million years, were subject to continuous pressure of overlying clay and silt deposition. This process lead to the petrification of the wood seen today. Upon closer examination, fossilized impressions of fish, amphibians and lacy ferns reveal that this fascinating region once thrived under swamp like conditions.

© Eldemira Portillo

A river of petrified logs cascade down this multicolored crevice in Blue Mesa.

An impressive conglomerate of clay, silt and sandstone formations, scattered petrified wood and giant boulders dominate the valley floor below Jasper Forest Lookout point.

# The Painted Desert

The Painted Desert located north of I-40 east of Holbrook, showcases the powerful effects of Mother Nature on the shale and sandstone mesas, buttes and washes. Sedimentation followed by geologic uplift subjected the exposed layers of rock to the ever present forces of wind, water and erosion to create the dramatic formations seen today.

© Eldemira Portillo

The Little Painted Desert north of Winslow is the creative masterpiece of millions of years of uplifting and the forces of erosion.

The Painted Desert at one of many lookout points.

# Grand Falls

Located 40 miles east of Flagstaff on Leupp Road is the largest waterfall in the state of Arizona. Grand Falls puts on a spectacular show in the spring when runoff from the snow melt in the North Country is at its peak. The rich mud-brown water as seen in this photograph is the result of the iron rich sediment picked up by the powerful scouring action of the water as it makes its way down the stream bed. The flow created by these massive falls, with a vertical drop greater than the world famous Niagara Falls, empties into the Little Colorado River.

# Coal Mine Canyon

Coal Mine Canyon named after the small coal mine located on the canyon floor, is located 14 miles east of Tuba City on SR 264.

From the overlook, one will experience an impressive display of formations intricately carved by the great forces of nature. Mineral laden rock combined with the ever changing light result in the vivid colors seen throughout the canyon walls. It is easy to see why Coal Mine Canyon is hailed as the most beautiful canyon on the Hopi Reservation.

# Window Rock

Window Rock, Capital of the Navajo Nation and seat of its tribal government, is named after the majestic sandstone window pictured here. The Navajo Nation is recognized as the largest and most refined of American Indian government. Eighty-eight Council delegates represent 110 Navajo communities throughout three states: Arizona, New Mexico and Utah. The elected tribal council meets in the council house located near the base of this natural formation. Also located at this site are the U.S. Government's Bureau of Indian Affairs, Navajo Area Office and the Navajo Veteran's Memorial Park. The Park honors the many Navajo soldiers who served in the military, noteably the Navajo Code Talkers, credited with helping the United States win World War II. Window Rock is located on SR 264 west of the Arizona - New Mexico border.

# Hubbell Trading Post

Hubbell Trading Post National Historic site located one mile west of Ganado on SR 264, is the oldest continuously operating trading post on the Navajo Reservation. John Hubbell bought the trading post in 1878 establishing himself as one of the leading traders of his time. Depicting the role of trading in the history of the Southwest and the life of a trader's family, business at the trading post is conducted much as it was in the 89 years the Hubbell family owned it.

© Eldemira Portillo

# Walnut Canyon National Monument

Located 7.5 miles east of Flagstaff on I-40 are the preserved remains of over 300 pre-Columbian dwellings built on a series of ledges along a 400 foot deep gorge. Inhabited by the Sinagua Indians, the architecture, in the form of alcoves consist of up to 12 rooms each with one outside entry as pictured here. Building underneath these cliff overhangs provided protection from both predators and the natural elements. Volcanic activity played an important role in the evolution of these remarkable people. Known to live as hunters and gatherers prior to the eruption of Sunset Crater, the Sinagua, after a series of vacancies, re-inhabited this area as farmers, indicating these ancient ones quickly adapted to an ever-changing environment.

These cliff dwellings are unique with respect to their environmental surroundings. Pinon-Pine habitat to the north and Sonoran Desert on the south facing slope are pictured here.

Wupatki National Monument located 30 miles north of Flagstaff off US Hwy 89A, is the site of the most extensive and best preserved ruins contained within this 35,253 acre monument. Wupatki consists of 13 excavated multilevel ruins once inhabited by the Sinagua Indians. Nalakidu meaning "Long House" contains 10 ground floors and several two-story rooms. Citadel ruin contains about 30 rooms and Wukoki an impressive three-story, eight-room ruin. Box Canyon Ruin (above) is one of the smaller Pueblos with the "sacred" snow-capped San Francisco Peaks rising majestically in the background.

Wupatki or "Tall House" pueblo is the most extensive ruin with more than 100 excavated rooms equipped with a ball court and an amphitheater. The excavation of weaving tools, cotton bowls and cotton seed reveal that textiles were a predominant trade item. Pottery shards, masonry and architecture indicate other native cultures; the Anasazi, Hohokam and Mogollon once inhabited this fertile region after the eruption of Sunset Crater.

# Flagstaff

© Eldemira Portillo

The area surrounding Flagstaff was inhabited by the Sinagua Indians as far back as the 1200's. The Coronado Expedition may have been the first white men to pass through the Northland in 1540 with the Spaniards making the journey 43 years later. The first wagon train lead by Lt. Edward Beale crossed Northern Arizona while making their way west in 1857. It wasn't until 1876 when the area's abundant springs brought in a surge of settlers. An adventurous group of Bostonians, in a show of patriotism fashioned a make shift flagpole from a young pine tree to fly the American Flag commemorating the nation's centennial. The "Flag Staff" remained while the Bostonians forged on, henceforth, the name "Flagstaff" stuck, appearing on documents relating to the Town. Flagstaff's first permanent settler and sheep man Thomas F. McMillian was soon joined by entrepreneurs Dennis and Timothy Riordan who formed the Arizona Lumber and Timber Company. Logging brought the railroad to Flagstaff which later brought David and William Babbitt to this booming logging and railroad town. Coming to the area to build cattle ranches and with the arrival of Charles, George and Edward the Babbitts formed the Babbitt Brothers Trading Company in 1889. The prominent Riordan and Babbitt families were instrumental in transforming this one-street Hamlet into the multicultural, technological and artistic mountain community.

Opposite Page: The San Francisco Peaks at the Northernmost entrance of Hart Prairie Road invites motorists to exit and explore this scenic back country.

# Lowell Observatory

This world famous observatory, founded in 1894 by astronomer Dr. Percival Lowell, is located 1 mile west of downtown Flagstaff atop Mars Hill. In 1915, Dr. Lowell predicted that an undiscovered planet named "Planet X" existed beyond the planet Mars. In 1916 Dr. Lowell died leaving the verification of this mysterious planet to a young resident assistant Clyde Tombaugh. Using a photographic plate he sighted "Planet X". The discovery of Pluto brought world wide acclaim to the observatory and the city of Flagstaff in 1930. (Right) The Slipher Building Rotunda, built to align with the rising and setting sun during the Spring and Fall Equinox.

(Above) This structure houses the 24-inch Clark Refracting Telescope. Once used for research, it's currently used for public astronomy lectures and viewing.

(Above) Dr. Percival Lowell's mausoleum was completed in 1923 at an astounding cost of $40,000. A lexan covering protects the translucent tile dome from weather damage.

# Historic Downtown Flagstaff

This picturesque tudor-style train depot located on Route 66 in the heart of downtown Flagstaff was built in 1926. Today, the train station houses The Visitor Center and continues to welcome passengers boarding Amtrak. This cross-country excursion train makes several stops here daily.

The Babbitt Brothers building named after the enterprising Babbitt brothers who settled here as cattle ranchers in 1886, operating a hardware store and launching the Babbitt Brothers Trading Company. The Babbitt building and historic Monte Vista Hotel, part of Flagstaff's colorful history, are located in historic downtown.

# The Pioneer Museum

Located 2 miles north of Flagstaff on Hwy 180, is the Arizona Historical Society's Pioneer Museum. Get a glimpse of daily life for Flagstaff's earliest settlers as you view the exhibits, memorabilia, and artifacts of old ranching and logging days. This two-story, turn-of-the century stone building, completed in 1908, once

served as the county hospital for the indigent. (Above) the 12-foot diameter "Big Wheels" were used by local logging companies.

Columbine (above) and lupine (right) are scattered throughout the pine forests surrounding Flagstaff.

# The Museum of Northern Arizona

Located three miles north of Flagstaff on US Hwy 180. The Museum of Northern Arizona, founded in 1928 by Dr. Harold Colton and his wife Mary, houses a variety of exhibits representing the biology, geology and anthropology of the Colorado Plateau. The Colton's interest in Native American arts and crafts led to the permanent collection and art shows that exhibit both traditional and contemporary works of art including jewelry, kachina dolls, paintings, pottery and rugs.

© Eldemira Portillo

© Eldemira Portillo

(Left) The McMillan House across from the Museum of Northern Arizona is the oldest home in Flagstaff. Built by homesteader and sheepman Thomas F. McMillan; Flagstaff's first permanent settler. Today, the McMillan house continues to maintain much of its historic charm.

# Williams & the Grand Canyon Railway

Located 30 miles west of Flagstaff on I-40 lies the small logging and ranching town named after mountain man Bill Williams, who guided trappers and hunting expeditions through this vast wilderness. Williams marks the beginning of the major entrance route to the Grand Canyon.

The Grand Canyon Railway, located at the Fray Marcos Hotel, takes passengers "back in time" as they embark on the 2 hour journey to the Grandest of Canyons. Beginning at the restored Williams train depot originally built in 1908, passengers board the restored 1923 Harriman coaches pulled by turn-of-the-century steam engines like the one pictured here from Pittsburgh, making the re-inaugural run on September 17, 1998.

(Below) A vintage photograph of Main Street.

# The Arizona Snowbowl

Located 7 miles north of Flagstaff on Hwy 180, the Arizona Snowbowl is distinguished as the most extensive ski resort in Arizona. With a vertical drop of 2300 feet, two double and two triple chair lifts, two ski lodges and cafeterias, a sports lounge and ski shop. For the cross country skier, the Nordic Center 17 miles north of Flagstaff on Hwy 180 offers 40 kilometers of groomed trails among the ponderosa pine, blue spruce and aspen-forests.

# Scenic Lakes of the Flagstaff Area

Upper Lake Mary located south of Flagstaff on Lake Mary Road is full year around and popular for boating, camping and fishing. Mormon Mountain pictured in the background is popular for camping and hiking.

Mormon Lake located further south on Lake Mary Road is the largest naturally occurring lake in the state of Arizona. Mormon Lake Lodge located at the west end of the lake is the site of many summer celebrations. The steakhouse and saloon is a popular hangout for Flagstaff natives and visitors alike.

The Beautiful snow-capped San Francisco Peaks reflect in one of many lakes surrounding Flagstaff. This photograph of Rogers Lake is taken after a heavy snow season.

# White Horse Lake

White Horse Lake south of Williams, is a popular camping and fishing hole surrounded by towering ponderosa pines. Take the Perkinsville Road east of Williams nine miles and turn left on White Horse Lake Road.

# Oak Creek Canyon

Oak Creek Canyon, fifteen miles south of Flagstaff on State Route 89A, was originally a cattle trail turned wagon trail by Jim Munds, a local rancher who used the trail as a short cut to Flagstaff. From the vista point at the top of the switchbacks to the city of Sedona, the drive offers a continuous display of changing beauty. As Oak Creek bubbles and cascades down the canyon it passes through richly diverse scenery. While the elevation of the canyon floor drops, ponderosa pines and fern, then sycamores and cottonwoods are followed by pinon and juniper covered canyons. Sheer cliff canyon walls are transformed into beautiful red rock formations as one makes their way into scenic Sedona.

Oak Creek Falls at Slide Rock State Park is a popular summer attraction.

Tranquil waters abound near Cave Springs Camp Ground.

# Scenic Sedona

The City of Sedona is nestled at the base of spectacular red sandstone formations 30 miles south of Flagstaff on Hwy 89a. The area known as Sedona began as a rural ranching community. It's natural beauty and rural feel caught the attention of Hollywood. Many western motion pictures, commercials and television shows brought national attention to Sedona contributing to its popularity. Named after the wife of T.C. Schnebly, one of the area's earliest pioneers who were instrumental in establishing the first Post Office. Today Sedona is considered one of Arizona's premier resort communities rich in art, culture, and history. For the outdoor enthusiast, trails abound in the area surrounding Sedona and Oak Creek Canyon. Many visitors and locals claim the beauty and energy of Sedona is inspiring.

(Left) Sunset brings a sense of tranquility to Red Rock Crossing south of Sedona.

# Chapel of the Holy Cross

Chapel of the Holy Cross, located 3 miles south of SR 179 on Chapel Rd, is wedged between 2 beds of Sedona's red rock sandstone. This concrete shrine built in 1956, offers visitors a panoramic view of the valley below and the more notable red rock formations of Courthouse Rock, Bell Rock and Cathedral Rock. The cross dominating the structure rises 90 feet high.

# Sedona's Treasures

Beautiful Bell Rock located six miles south of the "y" on SR 179 in the Village of Oak Creek, offers a peaceful respite to hikers and cyclists. Brilliant wildflowers, rabbits, gambel quail and an occasional coyote can be spotted while hiking the many popular trails.

Merry-go-round rock located on Schnebly Hill Road offers visitors a more extensive view of the Sedona area, Verde Valley and Mingus Mountain.

# Sedona's Rocks and Ruins

An early spring bloom adds interesting color to this scenic view near Lost Mountain.

Located near Sycamore Pass, this conspicuous sandstone formation housed a cave once used by a group of robbers seeking refuge from the law, hence the name, Robbers Roost.

Coffee Pot Rock is a prominent landmark in West Sedona.

Palatki is one of two large Sinaguan ruins located in the remote canyon walls southwest of Sedona. Situated at the base of a sandstone cliff, the architecture provided the Sinagua protection from the natural elements and predators. Drought conditions and hostile neighboring tribes may have lead to the abandonment of these remarkable cliff dwellings.

# Tuzigoot National Monument

This well preserved three story, one-hundred plus room stone fortress overlooks the Verde River Valley. Located 2 miles east of Clarkdale, Tuzigoot National Monument was home to the Sinagua who migrated here in the early fourteenth century. The site was abandoned during the same time period due to a high incidence of infant mortality. Much controversy exists among archeologists regarding the origin and final disposition of this remarkable tribe.

# Montezuma Castle

Montezuma Castle is an ancient Sinaguan Ruin occupied during the 12th century. Located 50 miles south of Flagstaff on I-17, this five-story, twenty-room limestone cliff dwelling sits high above the valley floor in an alcove surrounded by limestone cliffs and an overhang. Its prime location with Beaver Creek at its base provided water for farming indicating the Sinagua were highly adaptable to their surroundings. A smaller ruin can be found at Montezuma's Well located 10 miles north of Montezuma's Castle.

The Verde Valley is home to an abundance of desert wildlife including this coiled rattler ready to defend its territory.

# The Verde River Valley

The Verde River lazily winds its way through the Verde Valley and the town of Camp Verde. The Verde provides water for irrigation, livestock and recreational activities.

# Historic Jerome

The historic town of Jerome is located on SR 89A south of Cottonwood. Spanish missionaries exploring the Verde Valley noted that natives had discovered copper mines near what is now Jerome in 1583. These mines matched the description of the ones founded in 1883 by the United Verde Company. The mining camp was financed by Eugene Jerome of New York, who provided the camp be named after him. A smelter arrived by rail from Ash Fork in 1886 and the operation of this billion dollar copper mine began. Once a city with a population of 15,000 at the height of the mining boom,

Jerome became a ghost town when the United Verde Branch Copper Mines of the Phelps Dodge Corp closed in 1953. Today, Jerome with its unique shops, galleries, museums and studios is a popular tourist destination. Many restored buildings provide tourists a glimpse into its rich past.

(Top Left) A classic warning sign reflects the attitude of "ole mining days". (Top Right) The House of Joy on Main Street was once a house of ill repute.

The historic Little Daisy Hotel stands guard over a rustic remnant of the United Verde Extension Mine.

The town of Jerome today. The beautifully restored Jerome Grand Hotel perched high on the hillside was once a hospital.

# Prescott

Prescott, named after historian William Hickling Prescott, was first settled in 1864 by miners prospecting for gold. North of Prescott, the first seat of government, the state capitol was designated by President Lincoln because of the gold fields located there. The capitol was

then moved to Tucson only to be reclaimed by Prescott a year later in 1877. Twelve years later it again lost its title as capitol to Phoenix. Today Prescott is a resort community surrounded by the Prescott National Forest. Pristine mountain ranges, prairies and lakes offer a cool escape for neighboring desert communities. History, culture, education and a performing arts center add diversity while maintaining a small town feel. (Above) Historic Courthouse Square in its festive Holiday trim.

Bucky O'Neill Monument on Courthouse Plaza was designed by Solon H. Borglum, who also designed Mount Rushmore in South Dakota. The statue is a tribute to the first U.S. volunteer cavalry Captain William O'Neill during the Spanish-American War.

The Governor's Mansion was home to Arizona's first territorial governor, John N. Goodwin. Completed in 1864, the mansion houses period furnishings and artifacts dating back to Prescott's earlier days as a settlement.

# Rim Country

This rustic cabin of squared timbers and hand-quarried stone is one of many historical buildings lining the main street of Pine located 15 miles north of Payson on SR 87. Initially settled by the Mormons in 1879, today Pine is primarily an artists community.

The Mogollon Rim named after Juan Ignacio Flores Mogollon, the governor of New Mexico in the 1700's, rises over 7,000 feet above sea level and forms a massive escarpment that stretches 200 miles from North Central Arizona to west central New Mexico.

# White Mountain Region

Hawley Lake located on the Fort Apache Indian Reservation southeast of Pinetop ~ Lakeside, offers a wide range of outdoor recreational activities.

© Eldemira Portillo

A1 Lake located on SR 260 is an excellent fishing spot for locals and a convenient resting area for weary motorists amid the cool pine~ scented forest.

# Tonto National Monument

Located east of Roosevelt Dam on SR 188, Tonto National Monument preserves central Arizona's most accessible prehistoric cliff dwellings. What remains of a two-story, pueblo-style ruin is built in a natural cave that can be viewed from the park's headquarters. A one-half mile paved foot trail ascends 350 feet to this fascinating ruin once occupied by the Salado Indian tribe in the 13th and 14th century. Pottery and woven textiles were some of the artifacts left behind by this ingenious tribe. (Right) From inside the ruin, one can enjoy the panoramic views of the desert landscape and Roosevelt Lake in the valley below.

© Eldemira Portillo

The strategic placement of these cliff dwellings protected the Salado from neighboring tribes and the natural elements.

# The Salt River and Apache Trail

The Apache Trail at the junction of SR 188 and SR 88 near Roosevelt Lake was built in 1905 to transport supplies from Globe and Phoenix to the Roosevelt Dam site. The road parallels the ancient route of the Apaches through the Salt River Canyons. Apache Lake (Above) is the first of a series of lakes that meander along the trail as it makes its way to Apache Junction.

The Salt River meanders through the Salt River Canyon Wilderness Area, northeast of Roosevelt Lake on SR 288. Tubing down the Salt River is a fun way to cool off from the sweltering desert heat.

# Besh-Ba-Gowah Archeological Park

These seven hundred-year old pueblo ruins were once home to the Salado Indians. The availability of water, diverse food sources and climate made this an ideal settlement site. The Pueblo was built in stories; the ground floor was used for storage while upper floors served as living quarters. A roof hatch provided access to the rooftops where the Salado spent a majority of their time. Each structure could be entered through a central corridor perhaps for defense purposes or to channel all traffic to the central plaza, the center of commerce within the Pueblo. Parts of the original pueblo remain intact while others have been completely reconstructed. Artifacts excavated at the site and a ceremonial chamber showcase the daily life of the earliest inhabitants in this unique archeological village. (Right) Barrel cactus along with yucca and prickly pear grace the grounds surrounding the Besh-Ba-Gowah ruins and museum located near Globe, Arizona.

# Boyce Thompson Arboretum

© Eldemira Portillo

Nestled at the base of Picketpost Mountain west of Superior on US 60, is the Boyce Thompson Arboretum. Experience a natural showcase of towering trees, native and exotic cactus garden, a eucalyptus forest and hidden canyon. Founded by Col. William Boyce Thompson in the 1920's, a mining magnate, who was to use his great wealth to create the most useful and beautiful garden of its kind in the world. This 323 acre garden is Arizona's oldest and largest botanical garden. (Left) The cactus add interest to this otherwise barren rocky outcrop. (Below) A variety of desert succulents and cactus welcome visitors to the park's entrance.

© Eldemira Portillo

# Morenci

The Morenci Mine is the largest operating surface mine in the state of Arizona.

© Eldemira Portillo

The 127 mile, five-thousand-foot high byway connects the towns of Clifton/Morenci to Springerville/Eager. This historic route commemorates the journey of Spanish explorer Francisco Vasquez Coronado in search of the legendary Seven Cities of Cibola in 1548. As one travels the Coronado Trail, one will traverse the varied plant and animal life reflected in the area's extreme climb in elevation. Flat deserts are transformed into a series of rugged, dense, forest mountains, as one travels to the northeastern part of the State.

(Left) As the Coronado Trail climbs in elevation, tourists are treated to dense forests of oak, pine, fir and aspen.

The town of Alpine sits in a meadow surrounded by ponderosa pine in the the Apache-Sitgreaves National Forest.

# Arizona's Desert Landscape

Contrary to popular belief that the desert is nothing more than a dry, dusty, and barren environment, the Arizona desert landscape pictured here is transformed by the vibrant colors of wildflowers.

Interspersed with cactus, rocky outcrops and rugged mountains, the skeptic may find himself surrounded by some of the most spectacular scenery the southwest has to offer.

Springtime, particularly after heavy fall rains, showcases a multitude of yellow, orange, red, purple and white field flowers that cover the desert floor.

Brittlebush and lupine pictured here; Indian paintbrush, purple mat, Mexican poppy and evening primrose are the more common plant species.

Desert cacti common to Arizona's desert regions include saguaro (pictured), cholla, ocotillo, hedge hog, barrel and prickly pear cactus. The stately organ pipe cactus can only be found in a small portion of the southwest desert near the Arizona-Mexican border.

Bartlett Lake pictured here is guarded by giant saguaros and embellished by flowering shrubs. Take exit 223 from I-17 past Carefree.

# Lakes of the Sonoran Desert Region

Roosevelt Lake on SR 188, was impounded by the completion of Roosevelt Dam in 1910. Made with thousands of hand hewn stones, the dam is unique in that it is considered the worlds highest all-masonry dam. Lake Roosevelt, the largest of the desert chain lakes, boasts 112 miles of shoreline, is 25 miles long and up to 2 miles wide. When full, the lake is 349 feet deep at the dam, providing recreational activities for the outdoor enthusiast.

# Wickenburg

Wickenburg, named after Henry Wickenburg, a German immigrant and prospector was established in 1863. Wickenburg is credited with discovering the Vulture Mine yielding millions in gold, thus confirming Arizona's richest gold strike. Its blend of old western charm and rich mining heritage sets this rustic Sonoran town in a class of its own. With its ideal climate, dramatic scenery, exclusive guest ranches and world-class hospitality, Wickenburg has earned its distinction as the "Dude Ranch Capital of the World".

An abandoned assay office near the Vulture Gold Mine.

(Left) Main street of Wickenburg exhibits an "Old West" ambiance.

A dramatic sunset in the desert region surrounding Wickenburg.

# Hassayampa River Preserve

The Nature Conservancy's Hassayampa River Preserve is located on US Hwy 60 southeast of Wickenburg. Walk the many paths of this botanical garden along the Hassayampa River, called "the river which flows upside down" by the Native Americans. This unique river is considered one of the last natural riparian regions in the State. With its main flow 20 feet below the streambed, the Hassayampa, and its four-acre spring-fed pond/marsh habitat, is home to 230 species of birds. The preserve is designated by Wickenberg as its finest natural treasure.

# Lake Pleasant Regional Park

© Eldemira Portillo

Lake Pleasant Regional Park located 10 miles west of I-17 on SR 74, encompasses over 25,000 acres. Fed by the Agua Fria River, Lake Pleasant is impounded by Waddell Dam, an earthen dam 4,700 feet long and 300 feet high.

# Superstition Mountains

Located 5 miles northeast of Apache Junction on SR 88. These rugged mountains were named after the many legends surrounding them. The fabled "Lost Dutchman Gold Mine" lies hidden in these mountains. Whether it even exists remains uncertain. What is certain is that many men have died in search of it. Several monuments have been erected commemorating Jacob Walz, the man who purportedly discovered the Lost Dutchman Gold Mine.

# Phoenix – Arizona's State Capitol

Metropolitan Phoenix can best be described as a blend of eastern influence; with its sophisticat... high-rise office buildings and western lifestyle with its rambling ranch-style estates. Nat... American Pueblo and Spanish-Colonial architecture reflect the rich southwestern herita...

that sets Phoenix apart from the r... of its cosmopolitan counterpa... Prehistoric Hohokam India... probably the earliest inhabita... mastered life in this Salt Ri... Valley by building irrigat... ditches, mysteriously disappear... around the mid 1400's. A hay ca... established in 1864 by John Sm... supplied forage to Fort McDowell,... army outpost east of town. By 18... Phoenix became a supply post... the north-central Arizona territo...

With the mining boom in full force, saloons and gambling halls brought soldiers, miners and cowboys to town. Outlawry ran rampant prompting the need for law and order in those wild frontier days. The construction of the Roosevelt Dam, the Southern Pacific Railroad, the Central Arizona Project's aqueducts, and the advent of air conditioning played a key role in sparking the tremendous growth that ranks Phoenix the sixth largest city in the country. (Above) A conglomerate of historical and contemporary architecture create a dramatic skyline in Downtown Phoenix. (Right) The impressive Arizona State Capitol Museum a stone and granite Spanish-Colonial building served as the territorial Capitol from 1900 to 1912 when it became the state Capitol. As a museum it's restored wings exhibit artifacts and documents of early Arizona, Office of the Governor, Mining Inspector, Secretary of State and The House and Senate Chambers.

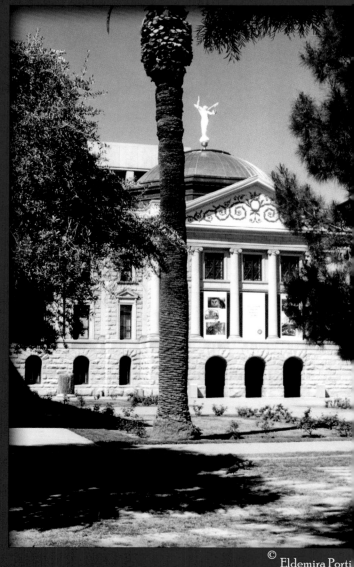

Central Avenue in downtown Phoenix is lined with executive high-rise buildings. Palm trees, flower terraces and water fountains hidden between these towering concrete structures play down their bold appearance.

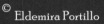

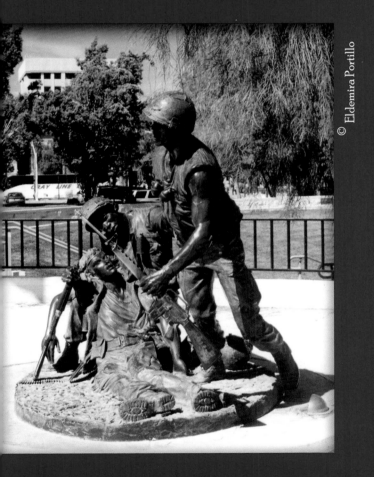

(Above)The Vietnam Memorial near the Arizona State Capitol honors local Veterans. (Right)The historic Hotel San Carlos opened in downtown Phoenix in 1928, the hotel is Phoenix's first high-rise. The Italian Renaissance design sets this grand hotel apart from neighboring structures. A recent multi-million dollar restoration preserves the historic character and charm ranking the Hotel San Carlos high on the National Register of Historic Places.

# Cosanti

(Left) This unique village in Paradise Valley blends desert landscaping with earth-formed concrete structures. Suspended among the courtyards, terraces and garden paths are a vast collection of bronze and ceramic windbells.

Designed by Paolo Soleri, an architect from Turin, Italy whose accomplishments include Arcosanti, the establishment of the Cosanti Foundation, the Soleri Windbells and numerous books. The sale of these magnificent windbells help fund the Cosanti Foundation whose mission is to combine architecture and ecology to produce a viable urban habitat.

# Pueblo Grande Museum

Walk the way of the prehistoric Hohokam as you stroll through these well-preserved ruins exhibiting rugs, pottery and figurines made from native material. A platform mound, ball court and irrigation canal reflect the ingenuity of the Hohokam in their attempt to adapt in the extreme desert environment.

(Right) Replicated pithouses share a common courtyard. Tools for making pottery and building materials are displayed on site.

# Fountain Hills

Named after the celebrated fountain in the town's park. The 562 foot tall fountain is said to be the largest in the world and shoots a magnificent spray every hour on the hour.

© Eldemira Portillo

© Eldemira Portillo

# The Heard Museum

Examine the architecture, culture and heritage of over 20 native tribes of the desert, uplands and the Colorado Plateau in the museum's permanent exhibit, "Native Peoples of the Southwest". Learn what it was like to live the native way by working on a bead loom or walking through a pueblo in the museum's interactive exhibit. The Heard is most noted for its impressive displays of Native American art, pottery, jewelry, basketry, rugs and Kachina dolls.

# Phoenix Sports

Bank One Ball Park: Home to the Arizona Diamondbacks baseball team, this dramatic structure located in downtown Phoenix has a retractable roof, restaurants, a picnic area and a swimming pool.

Glendale Sports Arena, Phoenix's newest state of the art sports arena, is home to the Phoenix Coyotes Hockey team. This imposing superstructure is lined with graceful palm trees. The entrance to the Arena is accentuated with towering water features and palm trees bringing a touch of elegance with its amazing evening light show.

© Eldemira Portillo

Taliesin West: this Frank Lloyd Wright architectural masterpiece located in Scottsdale showcases both indoor and outdoor spaces utilizing materials gathered from the desert floor. The lush desert vegetation and rugged land forms become an integral part of the design element further amplifying the natural beauty of this unique architectural jewel.

© Eldemira Portillo

© Eldemira Portillo

Rawhide is a tribute to Arizona's Western heritage, this 1880's authentic western town with its cowboy shoot-outs, gold-panning and Butterfield Stagecoach rides is located in Scottsdale.

# Casa Grande Ruins National Monument

The prehistoric Hohokam Indians built this four~story caliche~mud structure in the early 1300's. Casa Grande, the Spanish name for "Big House", represents the height of Hohokam architecture. The remains of a walled village and a ball court surround this massive structure. The steel umbrella was designed to preserve this fascinating ruin from the harsh desert elements.

© Eldemira Portillo

(Left) A colony of desert yucca grace southern Arizona's highways and byways.

# Florence

Founded by Levi Ruggles in 1866, Florence is one of Arizona's oldest towns. Many historic buildings and homes add charm to this rustic desert burg. Housing over 5,600 POW's during World War II, the Florence POW camp was the largest in Arizona. The Pinal County Historical Museum houses over 100 varieties of barbed wire, Indian artifacts and numerous documents chronicling the county's rich history. (Left) The Pinal County Courthouse lit by a fiery sunset is Florence's historic and architectural jewel.

One of many scenic desert highways, US Hwy 60, comes alive with color during the early spring months.

© Eldemira Portillo

# Picacho Peak

Picacho Peak State Park, 12 miles south of Eloy on I-10 is the site of Arizona's western most Civil War Battle. A dozen Union soldiers defeated seventeen Confederate cavalrymen on these grounds April 15, 1862. This 1500 foot peak was used as a major landmark for settlers traveling between New Mexico and California. The trails that meander throughout the park were the very roads constructed by the Mormon Battalion and used by the forty-niners as well as the Butterfield Overland Stagecoach.

# Saguaro Cactus

The saguaro cactus grows only in the low desert regions of Arizona. It can live more than two hundred years growing to a height of thirty to forty feet. It's blossoms appearing in May and June, is the Arizona state flower. The saguaro pictured resembles an arm carrying a bouquet of budding blossoms.

© Eldemira Portillo

A winding roller coaster road off I-10 takes visitors through 17,000 acres of rugged mountains embracing the largest stand of saguaro cactus in the southwest. The blooming of saguaro amidst a variety of desert wildflowers puts on a colorful show in late spring. An equally impressive stand of saguaro cactus can be found in the Rincon Mountain Park further east on I-10. (Left) Desert cacti combined with rugged rock walls and boulders provide exceptional photographic opportunities.

© Eldemira Portillo

(Left) Vibrant spring growth brings drama to the desert landscape south of Tucson.

# Sabino Canyon

This beautiful desert canyon lies east of SR 77 in the Santa Catalina mountains north of Tucson. It's steep rocky slopes dotted with saguaro cactus, surround the regions only continuous source of running surface water. The cottonwood and willow trees lining the stream bed offer a cool reprieve from the hot desert temperatures.

Hikers wade through the shallow pools in Sabino Canyon.

# Tucson

Tucson, located in the heart of the Sonoran desert, was founded on August 20, 1775 by Hugh O'Connor while serving in the Spanish army. He established the Spanish Presidio Wall, hence the nickname "Old Pueblo". The signing of the Gadsden Purchase in 1853 made Tucson a part of the United States, becoming the Capitol of the Arizona Territory only to lose its title to Prescott in 1889. Downtown Tucson, pictured here, reflects its Spanish heritage. Tucson is the second largest city in Arizona and the seat of Pima County. The high desert valley of Tucson is surrounded by Four Mountain Ranges; The Santa Catalina Mountains to the north, Rincon Mountains to the east, the Santa Rita Mountains to the south, and the Tucson Mountains to the west. One can certainly appreciate Tucson's interesting mix of history, culture and scientific diversity. Southern Arizona's deep-rooted Christianity is evident in its many chapels, cathedrals and missions in and around Tucson, notably St. Augustines Cathedral (above) with its ornate sandstone facade and twin bell towers, named after the Patron Saint of Tucson. The historic Pima Courthouse (right) is the site of Tucson's original walled presidio where a portion of the original adobe wall can still be viewed. With its many parks, museums, galleries, observatories and nationally-respected architecture, Tucson is truly a one-of-a-kind southwestern desert community.

© Eldemira Portillo

# The Sonoran Desert

© Eldemira Portillo

This dramatic sunset provides an ideal backdrop to these towering palm trees.

Mission in the Sun, south of the Santa Catalina Mountain foothills, was built by world renowned Tucson artist Ted De Grazia. Inside the quaint chapel are walls covered with the artist's murals. Next door, the Gallery in the Sun houses the most complete collection of DeGrazia's artwork.

# Arizona Sonoran Desert Museum

This internationally acclaimed zoo and desert botanical garden located in Tucson's South Mountain Park, exhibits more than 300 live animal species, including big horn sheep, a mountain lion, ocelot and birds in their natural habitat. Close to 2 miles of paved paths lead visitors through an impressive landscape exhibiting over 1300 species of plants and cacti indigenous to the Sonoran desert region. Seven pollination gardens showcase the interaction between insects, birds, bats and plants. Visit the limestone cave featuring Arizona's gems and minerals while learning about the geological processes contributing to the evolution of our planet.

© Eldemira Portillo

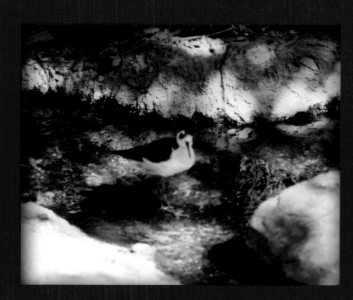

# Mission San Xavier del Bac

Eldemira Portillo

San Xavier Del Bac Mission on the San Xavier Indian Reservation in South Tucson is the finest example of mission architecture in the Southwest. Known as the "White Dove of the Desert", its brilliant white color poses a stark contrast to its surrounding desert environment. Founded by Jesuit Priest and explorer Father Kino in 1692, this Spanish Colonial Masterpiece was completed in 1797. The interior of the church houses multiple statuaries; God the father, Mother Mary, Mission Saints and Apostles. Designed by European artists using the finest of pigments, much of the historical integrity of San Xavier Del Bac remains intact. (Left) As seen from the mesquite ramada, the facade features Mexican-Baroque design. (Author's note: The left portion of the mission was undergoing extensive renovation. The photo taken used the mesquite post of this ramada to obscure the scaffolding that covered the left tower.)

(Left) Juices from the native prickly pear cactus were used as a base to produce the mortar used to build the mission.

# Kitt Peak National Observatory

Site of the world's largest concentration of telescopes for planetary, solar and stellar research. Kitt Peak's remote location at an elevation of 6,875 feet provide ideal conditions for viewing the night skies. Home to the McMath Solar telescope whose slanting shaft installation parallels the earth's polar axis at 32.5 degrees, is the largest of its kind in the world. Also on the grounds is the 158 inch Mayall Telescope whose scope is one of the four largest scopes in the nation. Over half the observing time is allotted to visiting astronomers and graduate students. Members of the Observatory's scientific staff occupy the remaining time slots.

© Eldemira Portillo

© Eldemira Portillo

(Above) An impressive list of universities in association with the National Science Foundation support and utilize the solar and stellar telescopes here at Kitt Peak.

(Right) The 158 inch Mayall Telescope whose light gathering power is equivalent to a million human eyes.

Organ Pipe National Monument in the remote Sonoran desert region southeast of Ajo on SR 85 is home to the stately organ pipe cactus. Intermingled with other desert cactus and rugged mountain terrain, these magnificent cactus sprout large lavender white flowers at night during the early summer months. Spring brings a brilliant show of

# Patagonia Lake State Park

Patagonia Lake, southeastern Arizona's largest lake located in the Coronado National Forest on SR 82, is popular for camping, fishing and boating. (Right) Boating enthusiasts spend the afternoon trolling the calm cool waters of Patagonia Lake. The wooden curved bridge welcomes boaters leaving and entering the marina.

(Below) Signs of remote civilization inhabiting the grasslands and rugged mountain ranges in southeastern Arizona.

© Eldemira Portillo

© Eldemira Portillo

© Eldemira Portillo

Madera Canyon and the Santa Rita Mountain range can be accessed from I-19 east of Green Valley. The road approaching the canyon winds through miles of golden swaying grasslands before ascending into the cool oak and pine forest canyon. Used by the area's earliest settlers for mining, logging, hunting and grazing, Madera Canyon's unique natural diversity provides the perfect habitat for an impressive number of bird species.

(Left) Acres and acres of windswept grasslands line the roadway leading to the canyon.

(Below) The Canelo hills and yucca line State Route 82 east of Patagonia.

# Tombstone

Tombstone "the town too tough to die" is the most renowned of Arizona's old mining camps. In 1877 Edward Schieffelin named his first claim, Tombstone after finding silver bearing ore veins in the hills surrounding this dusty desert hamlet. Soon stories of prospectors striking it rich caused this settlement to boom. The mining boom brought its share of lawlessness resulting in the infamous Earp–Clanton shoot out

©Eldemira Portillo

at the OK Corral. The Boothill graveyard at the edge of town serves as the final resting place of Billy Clanton, the McLowery's, John Heath and early settlers that shaped the history of Tombstone. (Above) Stagecoaches take visitors on a narrated tour of Tombstone's many historical sites. (Right) The New York Times ranked the Bird Cage Theatre as the wildest, wickedest nightspot between Basin Street and the Barbary Coast. One hundred and forty bullet holes adorn this opera house saloon. (Below) This weather beaten sign in front of the infamous Bird Cage theatre is a standing testament to the many gunfights Tombstone is famous.

Many of the towns' original structures have been restored and serve as fine restaurants, theaters and museums. Established in May 1880, "The Tombstone Epitaph" is the oldest continuously published newspaper in Arizona. The railroad depot now serves as the towns' public library. The Nellie Cashman Boarding House is now a restaurant and the Bird Cage Saloon, once a thriving gambling hall and bordello is now a museum. The original Bank of Tombstone now serves as a visitor information center. Tombstone is also home to the world's largest

rosebush. (Above) St. Paul's Episcopal Church established in 1882 is the oldest existing Protestant church in Arizona. (Right) Tombstone City Hall established in 1882 retains much of its historical charm.

(Lower Left) John Heath, along with his comrades who robbed and killed several townsfolk in a Bisbee store, were later lynched from a telegraph pole in 1884. (Lower Right) The historic Cochise County Courthouse, built in 1882 is now an Arizona State Historic Park.

© Eldemira Portillo

# Bisbee

This artist's colony on SR 80 is nestled in the Mule Mountains. With its turn-of-the-century charm, Bisbee was once a booming mining town in the late 1800's. During the mining rush, Bisbee's mines produced more than $2 billion in copper, gold, silver, lead and zinc. Once considered the largest cosmopolitan center between St. Louis and San Francisco with a population close to 24,000 at the turn of the century. Today, this bustling artists enclave boasts a population of about 6,500. Many of Bisbee's historic buildings are well preserved and serve as inns, art galleries, antique shops and fine restaurants. It's narrow winding streets lined with tall brick buildings echoes the architectural style of San Francisco.

(Bottom) This panoramic view of Bisbee shot on a late spring morning showcases the town's turn-of-the-century charm.

(Above) Art galleries and specialty shops line one of many narrow winding streets found in Bisbee's Historic District. Each building has its own special facade that gives this street its unique character.

# Douglas - Gateway to Mexico

Douglas was originally the site of cattle roundups for local ranchers, before later becoming a major copper smelting town. Today, this town serves as a center of commerce, manufacturing, agriculture and tourism. Many historical sites can be found around this quiet border town, notably the Gadsden Hotel. Built in 1907, this elegant hotel was destroyed by fire only to be rebuilt one year later in 1928. Designed by H.C. Trost, a well-known architect, the hotel is noted for its elegant lobby. (Right)

© Eldemira Portillo

With its Italian marble staircase, gold leafed pillars and 42-foot Tiffany stained-glass mural, visitors are easily transported to a by-gone era. Listed in the National Register of Historic places, the Gadsden Hotel is "the last of the Grand Hotels".

(Right) This "Colonial Revival" style house was built in 1908 by James S. "Rawhide Jimmy" Douglas, the city's namesake. The Douglas family originally from Canada, were prominent in the mining industry. In 1943, the home was purchased by Ben Williams. After an extensive renovation, the Williams family occupied the home until 1984. The home is now owned by the Arizona Historical Society.

# Gila River Valley and Mount Graham

The dramatic Gila River Valley and Roper Lake State Park south of Safford are both on US Hwy 191. The areas unique geology lures avid rockhounds in search of agate and chalcedony rose, while health enthusiasts enjoy the many mineral baths common to this area. (Below) The 10,720 foot summit of Mount Graham can be reached via the Swift Trail Junction also on Hwy 191. Travel through 5 of the 7 major ecological zones of the north western continent and visit Mount Graham's International Observatory housing the world's most powerful telescope.

© Eldemira Portillo

# Willcox

Willcox, "The heart of the Old West", is surrounded by rugged mountain ranges and miles of wide open space making it an ideal place for cattle ranching and agriculture. Most of this town's historical treasures can be found on Railroad Avenue. (Left) Rex Allen, the town's most famous character rose to fame in the 1940's as a country singer. A favorite tourist attraction is the Rex Allen Museum and Willcox Cowboy Hall of Fame located in Willcox's historic district

© Eldemira Portillo

The Southern Pacific Railroad Depot, constructed in 1880 is Arizona's only remaining redwood building currently housing City Hall. (Right)

© Eldemira Portillo

# Chirichaua National Monument

Known as the wonderland of rocks. Nowhere else in southeastern Arizona can one view a more spectacular show of granite spire formations. Interspersed with pinon pine, juniper and the distinctive red barked manzanita, one is truly awe ~ inspired at every turn in the road. A visit to the Faraway Ranch gives tourists a glimpse into the life of the Swedish family who were instrumental in establishing the area as a national monument. Take SR 186 southeast of Willcox to SR 181.

© Eldemira Portillo

# Tumacacori National Historical Park

Pimeria Alta, land of the Northern Pimas is the site of mission ruins located on I-10. The present church was built between 1800 to 1822 by the Franciscans. Father Eusebio Francisco Kino is credited with establishing Tumacacori in 1691.

Father Kino stopped at this O'Odham Indian village to celebrate mass, eventually colonizing the area and converting the Pima Indians to Christianity.

Tumacacori Mission is an architectural masterpiece built by the Spanish in 1882 using the native soil, gravel, limestone and timber from the Santa Rita Mountains. The brilliant white dome of the sanctuary stands guard over the cemetery in the back of this historic mission. The Bell Tower remains incomplete to this day.

# Nogales

This border town at the southern most end of Santa Cruz County is Arizona's most popular port of entry to Sonora Mexico. Bargain hunters come in droves to purchase Mexican arts, crafts and jewelry in Nogales, Sonora at prices considerably lower than those purchased in its' twin city north of the border. When visiting Nogales, you may want to view a few of the community's architectural wonders. (Right) The Sacred Heart of Jesus Parish sits perched atop a hill overlooking the historic district of Nogales. The Santa Cruz County Courthouse is at the heart of the historic district (Below). Across the tracks, the Pimeria Alta Museum showcases the rich heritage, culture and history of the beautiful Santa Cruz Valley. Poncho Villa; Mexico's notorious leading rebel eluded U.S. and Mexican authorities by hiding out in selected homes throughout the historic district.

© Eldemira Portillo

© Eldemira Portillo

117

# Kingman

Kingman, the seat of Mohave County, is in the "heart of" the longest existing stretch of Historic Route 66. Founded in 1880 by Lewis Kingman while surveying a railroad route between New Mexico and California, Kingman serves as an access point to

© Eldemira Portillo

lakes Mead, Mohave, Havasu and the Colorado River. Nearby Ghost towns; Chloride, Oatman and Mineral Park are living testament to Kingman's rich mining history. The Mohave County Courthouse (Above), the Powerhouse Visitor Center and Route 66 Museum (below) are just two of 62 structures in the community of Kingman listed on the National Register of Historic Buildings. One of Kingman's streets is named after its favorite son, Andy Devine, whose high squeaky voice landed him success in films, stage, radio and television.

© Eldemira Portillo

© Eldemira Portillo

Chloride, a nostalgic mining hamlet north of Kingman on US 93 is Arizona's oldest silver mining camp. The mountains surrounding Chloride are rich in silver, gold, lead, zinc and turquoise ores, Silver Hill holding the richest concentration of silver ore was discovered in 1862. During its heyday from 1900 to 1920, seventy-five mines were in operation. The escalating cost of material, labor and miners joining the military in World War II caused the mines to close in 1940. Today, Chloride with its rustic appeal is home to fine artists and craftsmen. Tony Mafia and Roy Purcell's murals (above) can be found in the neighboring Cerbat Mountains.

Eldemira Portillo

The Wild Roses, America's only all female gunfighters attract many visitors to Chloride. (Left) Arizona's oldest operating Post Office is located on Main Street, the only road into town.

# Lake Havasu City

Sprawled along the eastern banks of beautiful Lake Havasu is Lake Havasu City, originally an Army Air Corps landing strip and rest camp. Robert P. McCulloch purchased this arid land in 1963 hoping to turn it into a recreational and retirement community. In 1968, McCulloch brought England's London Bridge to this stark region. The bridge was dismantled brick by brick and reassembled on a man~made river channel bringing world acclaim to this hot desert oasis. Today Lake Havasu is the leading water sports mecca of Arizona. From sailing, water skiing, boat racing to excellent bass, catfish and bluegill fishing. Lake Havasu City is considered one of Arizona's top destination resort communities. (Right) London Bridge English Village is a popular tourist stop. (Bottom) Thousands of personal water craft navigate the London Bridge channel and open waters of Lake Havasu each year.

# The Parker Strip

From Parker Dam to Headgate Dam, towering palm trees, cattail coves and dramatic desert mountains line this magnificent 18-mile stretch of Colorado River Valley along SR 95. Wildlife, as diverse as the recreational opportunities inhabit this grand desert oasis.

© Eldemira Portillo

Bill Williams River National Wildlife Refuge, named after fur trader Bill Williams who explored the area in the 1800's. This 6,000 acre desert riparian and upland habitat is home to bighorn sheep, desert mule deer, bobcats, beavers and some

275 species of birds. Pictured is the confluence of the Bill Williams River and the Colorado River.

# Hoover Dam

Located on US 93, Hoover Dam, named after former President Herbert Hoover, was built by the Bureau of Reclamation to provide water storage, hydroelectric power and flood control support. Completed in 1936, it impounds Lake Mead, one of the nations largest man made lakes by volume. In 1938 the lake reached twenty-four million acre feet and extended one-hundred ten miles upstream. Designed by Gordon Kaufmann whose clean lines, shiny surfaces and monolithic design give the dam both a powerful and space age feel, Hoover Dam stands as a towering icon of one of the greatest engineering achievements in US history. (Below) A bronze scaffer pays tribute to the many men who worked tirelessly to make Hoover Dam a reality.

© Eldemira Portillo

© Eldemira Portillo